HOME
THEN AND NOW

by Robin Nelson

first step nonfiction

Lerner Publications Company · Minneapolis

Our homes give us **shelter** and keep us safe.

Homes have changed
over time.

Long ago, families used oil lamps for light.

Now, we use **electricity** to light our homes.

Long ago, families kept food
cold in **iceboxes**.

Now, we use refrigerators.

Long ago, kitchens had
wood-burning stoves.

Now, kitchens have electric
or gas stoves.

Long ago, homes had
outhouses.

Now, homes have bathrooms
with indoor toilets.

Long ago, families took
baths in tin tubs.

Now, families take baths in bathtubs.

Long ago, families washed
clothes with **washboards**.

Now, families use washing machines to clean clothes.

Long ago, children did
chores after school.

Now, we still have many jobs to do.

Homes Timeline

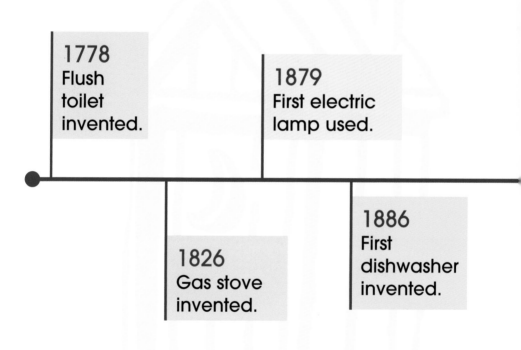

1778
Flush toilet invented.

1879
First electric lamp used.

1826
Gas stove invented.

1886
First dishwasher invented.

1908
First electric washing machine invented.

1947
First microwave oven used.

1891
Electric stove invented.

1899
Refrigerator invented.

1937
First automatic washing machine used.

Home Facts

 The first settlers in America built houses out of materials around them. Some settlers built log houses out of the trees nearby. Other settlers built sod homes out of dirt and grass. Settlers in the Southwest built adobe houses out of sand, clay, and straw.

 The first paper towels were invented to use in classrooms to prevent the spread of the common cold.